THE SKY'S THE LIMIT

ALL ABOUT THE ATMOSPHERE

MARK RAUZON

THE MILLBROOK PRESS   BROOKFIELD, CONNECTICUT

Published by The Millbrook Press, Inc.
2 Old New Milford Road
Brookfield, CT 06804

Photographs on pages 4, 6, and 7 courtesy of NASA. Photograph on page 8 courtesy of Johnny Johnson/ Alaska Stock ©1998.

Library of Congress Cataloging-in-Publication Data
Rauzon, Mark J.
The sky's the limit: all about the atmosphere / Mark Rauzon.
    p.   cm.
Summary: Introduces the atmosphere, discussing the purpose of each layer and how air, the sky, and weather are related.
ISBN 0-7613-1263-3 (lib. bdg.)
1. Atmosphere—Juvenile literature. [1. Atmosphere.] I. Title.
QC863.5.R38   1999
551.5—dc21   98-41600   CIP   AC

For Alex Knudtson

Earth from 22,000 miles away

A soft blue blanket of air called the atmosphere hugs our Earth. Gravity keeps the air from floating off into the frozen blackness of outer space.

Airglow reflecting on the lower atmosphere

   The sky's the limit for life. Without our sheltering sky, the thin film of life on our planet's surface would not exist. Sky-high layers of the atmosphere work together to protect us.

   Arcing over 350 miles above Earth is the layer called the thermosphere. This is Earth's heat shield. Sunlight is so intense in the outer limits of the thermosphere that temperatures can reach almost 2,000 degrees! Spacecraft traveling through this layer must have special heat-reflecting tiles for protection.

But shooting stars and old satellites burn up when they pierce the heat shield. Without the thermosphere, meteorites streaking across the sky at night would rain down like bullets.

Walking in space above Earth

The northern lights (aurora borealis) in the Alaskan winter

Below the thermosphere lies the ionosphere, 50 to 200 miles above our planet. In this layer, when sunlight hits air molecules, they shatter and release electrical energy called ions. We use the ionosphere for long-distance radio communication by bouncing radio waves off this energy field.

We can see the dancing and vibrating energy in the ionosphere when the northern lights sweep across the polar sky.

Under the ionosphere lies the mesosphere, about 30 to 50 miles up. Unlike the layer above it, the mesosphere is very cold, about 100 degrees below zero, because there are so few air molecules to absorb the sun's heat.

The stratosphere is below the mesosphere. This layer, 10 to 30 miles above Earth, is our sun screen. Here, a thin layer of ozone gas absorbs most of the damaging ultraviolet (UV) rays of the sun. But enough UV light gets through to cause our skin to burn.

The stratosphere is a windless, weather-less envelope of very thin air. We can see the setting sun paint the stratosphere pink and purple when the light bounces off vast amounts of vapor and dust here in the middle atmosphere.

Sunset in Corcovado National Park, Costa Rica

Mushroom thunderhead cloud, South Pacific Ocean

Below the stratosphere lies the thick air of the troposphere. This is our air supply and is the atmospheric layer where weather rules. It reaches only 5 to 10 miles up from Earth's surface.

At the top of the troposphere, huge flowing currents of air called jet streams rush around the world at about 200 miles per hour. Airplanes take advantage of the freezing cold jet streams and go with the flow.

Jet and contrail, Oakland, California

Sooty terns at sunset, Jarvis Island, Central Pacific Ocean

The jet streams push clouds around the globe, helping to shade the earth and recycle water. Clouds also reflect sunlight back into outer space, so not too much light hits the planet.

The sunlight that reaches Earth heats the land, which in turn warms the air. Warm air rises and cool air flows in to fill the void. The wind is the air whistling while it works. The moving air stirs the oceans, trims the trees, and sculpts the land.

Flagged tree, Wake Island ▶

Making a wish on dandelion seeds, Oakland, California

Wind carries pollen to fertilize plants, and carries flying seeds into faraway fields. It rolls tumbleweeds across the plains, spilling seeds as they go.

Spiders with parachutes and butterflies with beautiful wings float on the air. Birds ride the rivers of wind when they migrate.

Snow geese in Sacramento
Wildlife Refuge, California ▶

Breezes, blasts, gusts, or gales—an ocean of air flows around the world. The wind is always blowing somewhere on the planet.

Prayer flags on a Buddhist temple, Katmandu, Nepal

Wind-etched sand dunes in Canyon de Chelley National Park, Arizona

A chinook is a warm wind blowing down the Rocky Mountains. A williwaw is a blast of cold, wet wind in Alaska. A haboob is a blinding dust storm in North Africa. A mistral is a cold, dry wind in southern France, while a sirocco is a warm wind in the Mediterranean.

Waterspout over Puerto Arista, Mexico

Tornadoes, typhoons, cyclones, and hurricanes are the names of tremendous windstorms that can destroy everything in their path. Luckily, they happen only occasionally, but these events are important for life. Without them the air and water would stagnate.

When wind meets water, it pushes on the surface of the water and makes waves. As the waves flow across the ocean, water is stirred up.

Waves off Diamondhead, Hawaii ▶

Boobies and terns feeding, Central Pacific Ocean

As the surface water moves aside, water from the deep rises to the top. The deep water is usually rich in nutrients and oxygen, essential for life. Upwelling currents of nutrient-rich cold water make marine life abundant.

The oceans and forests help to freshen the air by adding oxygen and removing carbon dioxide. Plants and animals breathing in and out help make just the right mix of gasses.

Tree ferns near steam vent, Hawaii Volcanoes National Park

Hot air rising, warm rain falling, cool clouds rushing, and cold jet streams make up our air conditioning. The troposphere keeps our Earth in perfect balance for living things.

◄ **Flags and flying kites, Honolulu, Hawaii**

Sandhill cranes in flight, Los Banos, California

The sky is blue when the sun is shining because the air molecules absorb every color of the rainbow except blue.

But smoke from fires and fumes from cars and trucks make the sky brown.

Fire in Oakland, California, 1991 ▶

Air pollution traps the sun's heat, causing the earth's climate to slowly warm up. Like a greenhouse with its windows closed, Earth gets very hot in the sun. As the land heats up, the winds increase, causing more tornadoes.

The sky is also our umbrella, blocking out harmful rays of the sun. Chemicals we use every day can dissolve the ozone in the stratosphere and allow in more UV rays. Earth needs all the protection it can get from the sun's intense power.

Seven miles above the Central Pacific Ocean

Marching band horn player, Honolulu, Hawaii

Our air is our life. We can go months without food, days without water, but only minutes without air. We don't even have to think about it, for our bodies breathe automatically. Take a deep breath and share the air that is everywhere.